Elizabeth Castle
A Souvenir Guide

CW00449447

by Doug Ford

CONTENTS

Opposite – view of the Parade Ground and The Mount.

PRAISE THE LORD
AND PASS THE AMMUNITION . . .

In the mid-sixth century, Helier, a Christian from the town of Tongeren in the area we now call Belgium, arrived in the Island looking for solitude and a place where he could devote his life to prayer. It is said that he lived, for 15 years, on a small rocky outcrop on a tidal islet in the middle of St Aubin's Bay before he was killed by a band of sea rovers in 555 AD. Local folklore maintains that the murdered Helier picked up his severed head and carried it for two hundred yards. Such evidence of Helier's piety meant that he was popularly declared a saint and when the Island was split into parishes he was the obvious choice to be associated with the one closest to the site of his martyrdom.

St Helier's remote rock shelter became a place of pilgrimage and a small monastic community grew up on the islet, which was to last until the Vikings incursions of the ninth century. In 933 the Channel Islands were annexed by the newly founded Duchy of Normandy and became part of the diocese of Coutances. A procession is still organised by the Parish authorities, on or about 16 July – St Helier's day, during which a wreath is laid at the entrance to the twelfth century oratory which was built to cover the site of his rough dwelling.

When Henry Plantagenet, Duke of Normandy, married Eleanor of Aquitaine in 1152 the Channel Islands ceased to be simply on the periphery of Normandy as they were now on the route between his northern and southern lands. This new status was reinforced two years later when Henry became King of England because the Islands were on the main route between his possessions in England and in South West France. Henry tried to encourage the Islands to develop and so he encouraged the foundation of an abbey dedicated to St Helier on the small tidal islet in St Aubin's Bay. The actual founder was one of Henry's barons, William FitzHamon, who was to become Seneschal of Nantes in 1166 and Seneschal of Brittany in 1172. The Augustinian canons who lived there acted as scribes to anyone who needed their services, especially the growing numbers of merchants. Henry also granted the monks of the Abbey the watermill known as Le Moulin de la Ville and the area known as Le Marais de St Helier; and more importantly he gave them the right to establish a market. In 1179 the Abbey was downgraded to the status of a Priory when it was joined with the Abbey of Our Lady of the Vow in Cherbourg. Following its reduced status the number of monks fell and the influence of the Priory diminished; the last Prior, Jean Carvannell, was appointed in 1517.

All the religious houses set up in Jersey were connected with various mother houses on the Cotentin and because the church was seen as a non-political international body, the church in Jersey retained its links with the French mainland even after the political separation in 1204 when King John lost the Duchy of Normandy. However, whenever England and France were at war, one of the first things that was done was to prevent church revenue leaving the Island. When Henry V became King of England in 1413 he took over all property in the Island owned by foreign religious foundations, with the exception of the Priory of St Helier, which was to be closed by Henry VIII in the late 1530s.

St Helier Priory Church –
detail taken from Hollar's 1651 print.

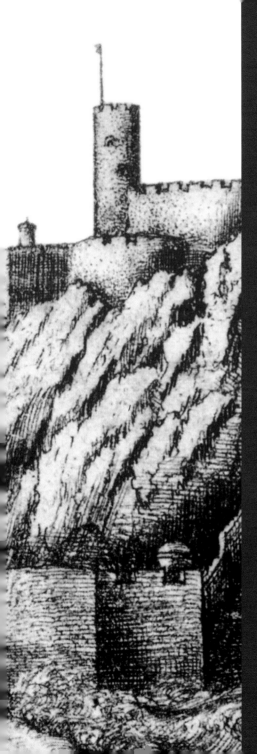

1406 PERO NIÑO RAID

In October 1406 a combined Franco-Spanish force led by Pierre Hector de Pontbriand, a Breton nobleman, and Pero Niño, a Castillian grandee, attacked the Island. Diaz de Gamez, Niño's standard-bearer, wrote an account of the raid in 'El Victorial', from which we can learn that the invasion force was composed of about 1,000 archers and crossbowmen, probably professionals from Normandy, Brittany and Castile. They made their base in the priory on the islet and fought an indecisive battle with a local 'militia' of 3,000 who had been drawn up along the facing sand dunes in the area around what is now People's Park and the Grand Hotel. The militia advanced on the invaders and the battle raged fiercely with hand-to-hand fighting until the rising tide forced the sides apart. Overnight Niño learned of the defences of the Island, which coupled with what he knew of the militia's capabilities made him switch his strategy to one of terrorism. The following day detachments were sent out to pillage and destroy whatever they could find but were told to avoid a pitched battle. This they succeeded in doing apart from a skirmish at the top of Grouville Hill (La Croix de la Bataille). The new strategy had the desired effect on the militia: unwilling to allow this destruction of their property and suffering to their families to continue the Islanders agreed to pay a ransom of 10,000 gold crowns to the invaders in return for their departure.

We can also deduce from this account that in times of danger the Islanders did not go to Mont Orgueil Castle at Gorey, but tried to place their families in places of refuge such as Chastel Sedement in Trinity or at the old Iron Age promontory forts at Rozel, Frémont and Grève de Lecq.

A Castle for a Queen

Once gunpowder and cannon were introduced into warfare it became obvious that, despite attempts to upgrade its defences, the old medieval castle of Mont Orgueil at Gorey on Jersey's east coast, was no longer up to the job of defending the Island. This was especially true once the size of merchant ships grew to the extent that they needed a secure anchorage and so in 1551 Sir Hugh Paulet built a small battery to be manned by six gunners on the highest part of the islet – the Mount – to protect the haven of St Helier and, along with the tower at St Aubin, the anchorage in St Aubin's Bay. It soon became apparent that these batteries were not sufficient and the tower at St Aubin lacked room for expansion and so further work was planned in the area of the islet we now know as the Upper Ward or Mount. In 1594 Paul Ivy, a Crown Engineer, was appointed to carry on the work of fortifying the Upper Ward. The entrance to this new castle, the Queen Elizabeth Gate, bears the arms of Sir Anthony Paulet (Governor 1590-1600) while the Captain's house carries the date 1594 on its chimney.

The Haven of St Helier painted in 1545 shows the Priory Church buildings and the Hermitage Chapel. © British Library

After six years of building the New Castle, as it was referred to, was re-named Fort Isabella Bellissima - Elizabeth Castle - in honour of the Queen, by Sir Walter Raleigh who was Governor between 1600 and 1603. Virtually as soon as the castle was completed it was decided to build another gun platform in front of the main gate. This extension, entered through the new Iron Gate is known as Ralegh's Yard although whether it is named after Sir Walter Raleigh or George Ralegh, who was Lieutenant Governor in 1661, is uncertain.

Between 1626 and 1636 the Mount had a tall lookout tower added to it and the castle was extended to enclose the flat land on which the old monastic buildings stood. These new walls were over six metres high and the remains of the old Priory Church were used as a magazine and storeroom. Outside the new main Guard (the Third Gate) the storm beach, which separated the two islets, acted as a ditch. This was the castle that was held for the King by Sir Philippe de Carteret and then his nephew George Carteret throughout the English Civil War.

Paul Ivy's plan of 1594 shows the raised circular area of the Mount carrying four guns and the lower area with ten guns positioned along its walls. © British Library

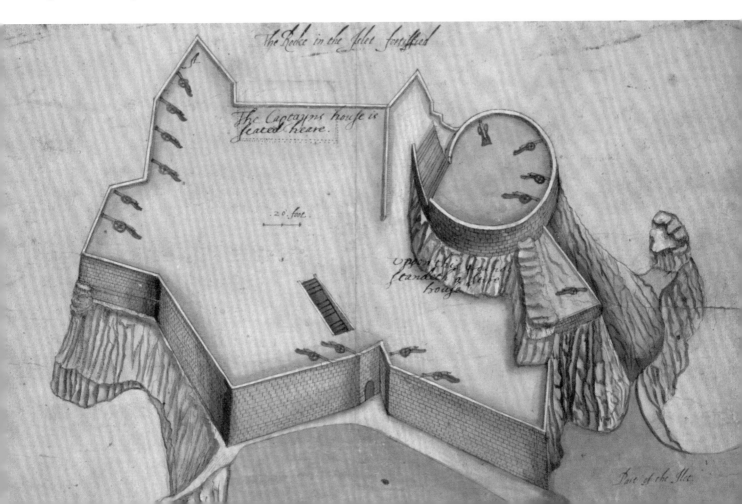

THE ENGLISH CIVIL WAR

At the outset of the Civil War in 1642 the King's Party within the Island was headed by Sir Philippe de Carteret, the Seigneur of St Ouen, who held the positions of Lieutenant Governor and Bailiff.

Hostilities broke out in the Island in March 1643 when de Carteret tried to read a letter from the King to the States. He was prevented from doing so and withdrew to Elizabeth Castle when he learned that the St Clement and St Saviour militias were marching on town to arrest him. Throughout April the castle garrison continued shopping in town while the townspeople barricaded the streets leading to the shore. War broke out in reality at the end of that month when Elizabeth Castle guns fired on some Parliamentary ships which attempted to shelter in the lee of the castle.

From May 1643 the garrison had to rely on Sir George Carteret to supply them by sea from St Malo. In July some form of sickness broke out amongst the garrison and on the 29th, Sir Philippe's son Gideon died and by mid-August Sir Philippe, himself, was on his deathbed. Following the death of Sir Philippe in August 1643 the King appointed Sir George Carteret, Philippe's nephew and son-in-law as Lieutenant Governor and Bailiff. He managed to expel the Parliamentarian faction and the Island was held for the King until 1651.

During this period the Island provided shelter for members of the Royal Family. Between April and June 1646 the Prince of Wales and his brother the Duke

of York, arrived in the Island and took up residence at Elizabeth Castle while their entourage was billeted in the town area. A revue of the Island Militia was organised and for a short time the entire Island appeared loyal to the cause. A second visit between September 1649 and February 1650 saw the return of the Prince, now King Charles II, to Elizabeth Castle along with a host of impoverished supporters. Charles had been proclaimed King in Jersey the previous February, as soon as news of the execution of his father, Charles I, reached the Island. The reason Charles II came to Jersey this second time was that of all his dominions only Jersey was a safe refuge for him. Obviously this act of loyalty would have its consequences.

The end for Royalist Jersey was inevitable and in October 1651 an invasion force of eighty vessels sailed for the Island carrying Colonel Heane's regiment, six companies of Hardress Waller's Regiment of Foot and two troops of horse – over 2,500 seasoned troops escorted by Admiral Blake's fleet. To these were added another 900 troops from Guernsey.

The unenthusiastic Jerseymen melted away and the veterans of Cromwell's New Model Army controlled the Island. The Royalist garrison withdrew to the castles and Blake was able to anchor his fleet in the bay, out of range of the Elizabeth Castle guns.

Below left - Elizabeth Castle viewed from the west. Wentzel Hollar, 1651.

Below - Elizabeth Castle viewed from the east. Wentzel Hollar, 1650.

Mont Orgueil Castle surrendered after a three-day siege but Elizabeth Castle was a more formidable task, both because of its position and because Sir George himself commanded the garrison. However, Heane imported three great 15-inch mortars from Portsmouth. These were positioned on the closest part of St Helier and launched a steady bombardment. One of the shells crashed through the roof of the old Priory Church, which was used as a powder store, and the explosion destroyed two years supplies of food and powder and resulted in forty casualties. It literally knocked the stuffing out of the defenders. On 24 November Carteret sent a messenger to the King in Paris to ask for new supplies and further instructions. The impoverished King could only advise surrender on the best possible terms available.

Negotiation lasted for eight days and Carteret managed to come away retaining his freedom and all his own property, his widowed sisters kept their estates and the garrison was allowed to march out with all the honours of war. His supporters, however, had to forfeit two years income to retain their estates.

On the 15 December 1651, Carteret signed the surrender document and finally the English Civil War could be said to have finished with a Parliamentarian victory. Castle Cornet in Guernsey, which had been an outpost of Elizabeth Castle, deprived of its supply base now had no hope of continuing its lonely struggle and so was forced, as a result of the action in Jersey, to surrender after nine years of siege.

Elizabeth Castle viewed from the north. Wentzel Hollar, 1651.

Elifabeth Castell in Iarfey.

Built to house artillery, the castle had 15 cannon during the siege of 1651, while in 1783 there were 84. The largest were 24-pounders like these, however, by 1804 the largest were 68-pounders.

During the Civil War the Castle was extended a third time when a number of modifications were made to the castle's defences. An outpost known as Fort Charles was built at the northern end of the islet commanding the approaches to the castle and in 1651 this was backed up by a fortified windmill built on the site of what was to become the Second Gate.

The problem of the undefended northern part of the islet was solved in 1668 when a fourth extension of the castle was undertaken and the entire islet was surrounded by a curtain wall. As a result the storm beach that cut the islet in two was turned into a ditch. At about the same time, a gun battery housing three cannon was built on top of the Hermitage Rock to act as an outpost on the seaward side.

During the first half of the eighteenth century the Lower Ward was extensively remodelled especially by the engineer, John Henry Bastide. The Parade Square assumed its present layout when the last remains of the Priory Church were removed in 1735. New barracks were built for both officers and men, as well as an Ordnance Store, Canteen and Prison Cells. After 1749 little new building work took place in the eighteenth century. When the Grand Battery was re-modelled in 1770 to take fifteen 24-pounders it became necessary to create new magazines for gunpowder and these were built into the walls of the ditch.

Above King Charles II taken from a 1662 charter.

The Battle of Jersey, 1781

Elizabeth Castle is surrounded by the sea for seven hours out of every twelve and while this was originally seen as a strength it also turned out to be a weakness because it meant that any troops garrisoned here were unable to be used effectively to defend St Helier when the causeway was covered by the tide. This weakness was highlighted in 1781 when the French landed at La Rocque and successfully occupied the town and captured the Lieutenant Governor, Moise Corbet, in bed. A party of French soldiers accompanied Corbet to the castle but were repelled by cannon fire. Corbet's written order to surrender, delivered under a flag of truce, was ignored by Captain Mulcaster, the officer in command of the castle. He simply stuffed it, unread, into his pocket, explaining to the French officer that he did not understand French. By the time Pierson arrived from St Peter with his troops the tide was in, and so

Mulcaster's "invalid" battalion were unable to participate in the battle. As a result of this invasion a review of the Island's fortifications was undertaken and, as a consequence, a new fortification was built above St Helier on Mont de la Ville – Fort Regent.

Right The Battle of Jersey by EF Burney.

Left The leader of the French forces, Baron de Rullecourt.

During the Napoleonic War a Hospital Block was built straddling the Traverse Wall in the Outer Ward. However, Elizabeth Castle's days as the Island's main fortress were numbered and in 1814 the new fort on the Mont de la Ville, Fort Regent, was completed.

Elizabeth Castle carried on as an army garrison until 1923 when it was sold by the British government to the States of Jersey for £1,500 to be used as an historic monument. It resumed its former role briefly during the Occupation when the Germans, using Russian and other forced labourers, refortified the castle and used it as one of the strongpoints in St Aubin's Bay commanding the sea approaches to St Helier. It was divided into a northern sector and a southern sector, which were manned by an infantry unit with support from Luftwaffe personnel who manned the anti-aircraft guns. The garrison of three NCOs and 34 men were housed in the Officers' Quarters and the Governor's House and their kitchen was in the Ordnance Store in the Lower Ward. The castle was also used as a punishment camp by the TODT Organisation for the forced workers who tried to escape from the other camps. In the course of the Occupation many of the buildings in the castle were stripped of their internal fittings and timber to be used in the soldiers' stoves.

After the Liberation, thirty skilled German prisoners of war were kept on the Island to clean the site up and to carry out a programme of repairs and restoration and when the Jersey tourism industry started up again, the castle became one of the Island's major tourist attractions.

A castle in the 21st century

Today the castle is administered by Jersey Heritage. Great care is taken to ensure that materials selected for repairs are as close to the originals as possible and traditional techniques are used where appropriate. Visitors approach the castle from West Park. At low water, the falling tide uncovers a causeway that follows a shingle ridge out to the castle for about 2½ hours either side of low water while at high tide there can be in excess of six metres of water over the causeway and so access is via amphibious vehicles.

The crew of a German field gun carry out a drill on the Albert Pier. Elizabeth Castle in the background

TOUR OF THE CASTLE

Elizabeth Castle is essentially divided into three different areas; the highest and oldest part is called the Mount or the Upper Ward; and beneath this is the Lower Ward, which contains many eighteenth century buildings; and finally the Outer Ward.

Right – The early morning view from the East Bastion over Le Havre de Saint Jaume.

OUTER WARD

Protected on both sides by projecting bastions, the Main Gate to Elizabeth Castle, or the Landward Gate as it was sometimes referred to, was built in 1668 when a curtain wall was built to completely encircle the islet. Usually the construction of an important gateway in a Royal castle would be marked by the inclusion of the Royal Coat of Arms and those of the Governor and his Lieutenant in recesses. Here at the Elizabeth Castle the recesses stand empty – testament to the parlous state of Charles II's finances.

Inside the Main Gate, set into the Western Wall which was built in 1668, is the original Port Guardhouse which now houses the modern-day ticket office. This was re-modelled in 1755 but in 1810 this was replaced with a new guardhouse, complete with a cell, built on the raised level opposite to the rear of the Gate Battery.

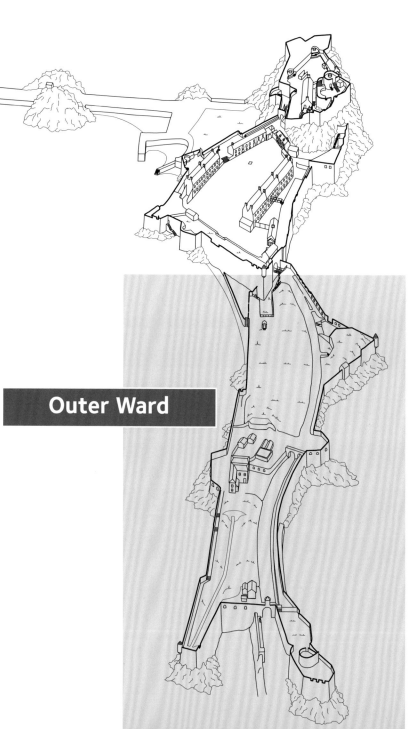

Outer Ward

From the Main Gate the roadway goes straight towards the Lower Ward through the Second gate and then across the Green to the Third Gate.

The Guardhouse was manned by the duty officer and a senior NCO on a 24-hour rota. They ensured that the guard on the gate and sentries on the walls were periodically relieved and supervised. As the Main Gate is the only practical access for wheeled transport and visitors on foot, the gate guard was responsible for checking credentials and turning away suspect persons or foreigners. The cell was where drunken or otherwise recalcitrant soldiers returning from town were held before being disciplined.

Above - The 1810 Guardhouse.

Behind the 1810 Guardhouse stands the Gate Battery. Sited on the 1668 curtain wall linking Fort Charles and the North East Bastion, this had four embrasures through which cannon were able to command the approach to the castle over the causeway. In 1680 these cannon were described as two demi-culverins[1] and two sakers[2]; they were eventually replaced in the eighteenth century by much larger 24-pounders. During the Occupation the Germans mounted a Czech-made 4.7 cm anti-tank gun in a timber lean-to here, and the date 1944 can still be seen in the concrete just above the gun. This was partially demolished in the clean-up after the Liberation and all that remains today are the rails and the ball mounting in the modified opening through the wall.

The belfry built above the Main Gate housed the bell that was rung to warn the garrison that the causeway was about to be covered by the tide and the castle would be cut off. Soldiers who missed the tide had to report to the Piquet House built at West Park on the landward side of the causeway. Failure to do so meant court-martial. Elizabeth Castle is surrounded by sea for seven hours out of every twelve. While this was initially seen as a strength, it also turned out to be a weakness because it meant that any troops garrisoned here were unable to defend St Helier when the causeway was covered. This weakness was highlighted during the

Battle of Jersey in 1781. The belfry was constructed just after 1840 and until that point a drummer beat the 'Pioneers March' around the Parade Ground and then down to the Port Guard before returning to the Main Guard (now known as the Third Gate) to warn everyone in the castle that the causeway was about to be covered.

From the Gate Battery follow the wall along to the right to reach the North East Bastion. This was sometimes referred to as the Lower Meadow Bastion because the area between here and the Hospital Block and the Traverse Wall was used by the garrison to grow vegetables to supplement their rations. Built in the 1730s it originally had four

cannon, which could provide flanking fire across the approaches to the Main Gate, but these had been reduced to two by 1783. The paving stones here are unlike the local granite and may be those mentioned as being shipped into the castle from Swanage in Dorset in 1647 at the time Fort Charles was being built. The bastion has one of the castle's distinctive 'pepper pot' sentry boxes which were probably built in the 1730s by John Henry Bastide. The decorative ball on the lead roof was replaced in 2006 and is based upon an 18th century engraving of the castle. During the Occupation part of the parapet was cut down when the Germans used the bastion as a floodlight position from where a 90 cms floodlight could illuminate the Inner Roads and the approach to the Harbour. The light was stored in a specially built bombproof shelter, which was dug into the Soldiers' Garden next to the Hospital Block. The shelter was linked to the North East Bastion by rails.

From the North East Bastion the visitor is faced with a choice as there are two different ways of reaching the Green – the western route goes via Fort Charles and the Wall Walk through the Second gate to the West Bastion and then onto the Green while the eastern route goes via the Gate in the Green to the East Bastion and around the Hospital onto the Green.

Far left - The belfry.
Left - One of the distinctive 'pepper pot' sentry boxes.

THE WESTERN ROUTE

From the North East Bastion retrace your steps to the Belfry and then carry on over the Main Gate. Fort Charles was built here over the winter of 1646/47 during the English Civil War and named in honour of the Prince of Wales (later King Charles II) who was resident in the Island at that time. It was built as an outlier to defend the approach from the causeway and to protect the castle by preventing an enemy gaining a foothold on the northern end of the islet.

Because it stood outside the original castle it had to be a self-contained unit and so a ditch was dug across the narrowest part of the islet, which was crossed by a drawbridge and fronted by an eight feet (2.4 m) high wooden palisade. Inside the fort was a small barrack building, sometimes referred to as a tower, which was accessed by a doorway in the west side, and a battery of five or six cannon. In 1668 when the curtain wall was built around the islet, Fort Charles became part of the main castle but it retained its own ditch and drawbridge until about 1750 when the ditch was filled in.

Above - Fort Charles.

Below - Fort Charles in 1922.

During the Occupation a machine gun position was set up on the north side of the battery and another was sited on the top of the tower.

In 1680 it was armed with two minions[3] on its south west side which could shoot along the face of the curtain wall and a demi-culverin and two more minions facing northwards to cover the approaches to the castle while a saker was mounted on the roof of the tower.

Above – The Hospital Block seen from the North West.

From Fort Charles follow the Wall Walk along to the Second Gate. This gate is set into a Traverse Wall which divides the Outer Ward in two. It was possibly built just after the 1668 curtain wall as it is shown on a plan drawn up in 1680. Although this wall was never shown as a single line of defence and was often associated with a pair of parallel walls running down to the Main Gate and

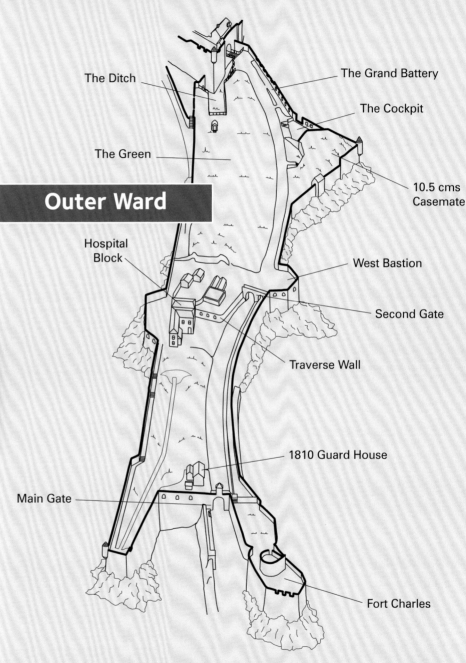

Outer Ward

The Ditch

The Grand Battery

The Cockpit

The Green

10.5 cms Casemate

Hospital Block

West Bastion

Second Gate

Traverse Wall

1810 Guard House

Main Gate

Fort Charles

Fort Charles, it did have gun embrasures cut into it so it served as a support line for the Main Gate. About 1697 it must have been modified or rebuilt for the Second Gate was remodelled and had three Coats of Arms set above it - as one views them, those of King William II are flanked to the left by those of Thomas, Lord Jermyn, who was Governor between 1684 and 1704, and to the right by those of Colonel Collier, who was Lieutenant Governor between 1695 and 1715. In the nineteenth century the south side of the gate arch was replaced in brick and the parapet lowered but perhaps the most intriguing modification happened during the Occupation when the jambs were cut back about 15 cms on each side in order to widen the roadway. It is said that it was done to enable lorries to pass through the gate but given the massive work undertaken by the Germans it would have been simpler had they just demolished it.

A plan of 1737 shows that a limekiln had been built on the north side of the Traverse Wall to replace an older kiln close by. The lime produced here would have been used in the reconstruction work in the castle for it had been found that earlier builders had used loam as a mortar to bind the stone together which meant the walls had to be strengthened by having massive batters or masonry aprons added to their bases. Next to the limekiln were the stables. Both of the features, along with part of the Traverse Wall, were lost in the early years of the nineteenth century when the Hospital Block was built.

At the end of the Wall Walk a narrow doorway protected by a gun embrasure allows the visitor to pass into the West Bastion. This arrowhead-shaped bastion was built in 1668 and Philips[4] in his plan of 1680 shows that it contained six cannon - one minion and

five sakers – and that by 1737 the 'pepper pot' sentry box had been built onto the projecting angle. In addition to the cannon embrasures, set into the walls are small musket loops through which the garrison could shoot along the face of the curtain wall while totally protected. During the Occupation another light automatic gun was positioned in the bastion but this was demolished in the clear up.

Left - The Hospital Block from the South East.

Top - The Cannon embrasures and musket loops of the West Bastion.

Above - Close up of the musket loops which pierce the walls of the West Bastion.

On the other side of the roadway, on a rock outcrop stood a fortified windmill, which was built in 1650 or 1651 just before the castle was beseiged by a Parliamentarian army from England. As a building, it had a dual purpose. The windmill was used to grind corn into flour for the garrison's bread while the lower storey had loop-holes cut into the walls through which muskets could be fired. This meant that soldiers stationed here could support those in Fort Charles to prevent or delay any potential invaders gaining a foothold on the islet. However by 1680 the curtain wall and the Traverse Wall had been built, which rendered the windmill obsolete and it had been demolished by 1737.

THE EASTERN ROUTE

From the North East Bastion follow the curtain wall up to the East Bastion. There is a step in the alignment of the wall which allows a splayed opening for a cannon to be set into the wall.

Above the Searchlight Bunker the imposing Hospital Block was built straddling the Traverse Wall in the latter years of the Napoleonic Wars. The initial phase, built in 1810, consisted of a two-storey building with two wards (one for enlisted men and a separate one for officers), a surgery, washrooms and a kitchen. Shortly after, a single storey extension was added to the south which included an infectious ward and a mortuary or 'dead house'. Before this building was erected there was a hospital somewhere in the castle as it was mentioned in Standing Orders issued in 1771, however, its location is unknown. Behind the Hospital Block and the Traverse Wall an engineers' store and stables were built along with a coal store.

The East Bastion, also known as the Upper Meadow Bastion built in 1668 and shown in Philips plan of 1680, was designed to take six cannon. It was possibly remodelled by John Bastide in the early 1730s. There are two-gun embrasures on each of its faces and those to the south have a clear view over the small sandy bay which was the

Top - The view from the North East Bastion along the East curtain wall towards the Hospital and East Bastion.
Right - The Green.

site of the castle's (and St Helier's) first harbour – Le Havre de Saint Jaume. In 1685 Dumaresq[5] wrote that ' . . . *there is a small pier unfinished under the castle walls at the east side by a sally port, where the castle boats are usually kept, and where greater vessels may be safe; but the entrance is narrow and dangerous, though good enough for boats.'*

The narrow path between the Hospital and the curtain wall is the site of the Gate in the Green. Passing through one enters onto the Green where at this point the two suggested routes come back together.

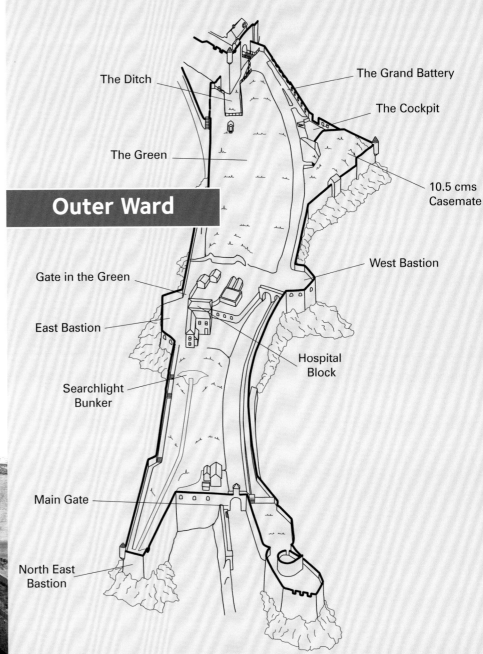

Outer Ward

The Ditch

The Grand Battery

The Cockpit

The Green

10.5 cms Casemate

Gate in the Green

West Bastion

East Bastion

Hospital Block

Searchlight Bunker

Main Gate

North East Bastion

"... in all Pride of Security, stands Elizabeth Castle, a Fortress mounting nearly one hundred Pieces of Cannon ..."

J Stead, 1809

The Green

In the 1640s when this area was outside the castle walls there was a bowling green here. Following the Restoration in 1660, Charles II recognised the inherent weakness in having such a large area undefended and so, in 1665 he ordered the Governor, Sir Thomas Morgan, to ensure that the Island was protected from invasion and he allocated £2,000 'to the defence of the bowling green'. This was the construction of the curtain wall and its associated bastions which meant that by 1668 the entire islet was fortified. Despite its length between the Gate on the Green and the Lower Ward there were only four gun embrasures in its entire length, one was lost when the Germans built the personnel bunker, one is about one third of the way along its length and the Two-Gun Battery is sited next to the East Sally Port in the Ditch.

Set back from the curtain wall, but running parallel to it, the Long Barracks were built around 1690-1700. This provided accommodation for four companies (at this time a typical company would consist of about 80 officers and men). The quality of the build left much to be desired as it was described as an 'Old Pile' in 1737 and as 'greatly decayed' in 1755. It was mentioned as late as 1783 but was demolished soon after and today nothing remains of it. The northern end would have been destroyed in 1942 when the Germans constructed a fortress standard[6] personnel shelter with twin entrances and two rooms, one for ten men and one for stores.

On the seaward side of the Green stands a Jäger type coastal casemate for a 10.5cms cannon. The gun, a Schneider captured from the French and brought over to the Island, had a range of twelve kilometres which means it could effectively shell Corbière. Originally these bunkers would have been lined with wood and the ceiling was supported by steel girders and steel plates which prevented concrete being dislodged during a bombardment. The gun crew were able to sleep in the bunker as there were bunks attached to the walls of one of the rooms.

To the south of this gun position is an area known as the Cockpit which now houses the 6-pound gun used by re-enactors as part of their display. It was created during the Occupation when about half the Grand Battery was filled in to create a searchlight position. In 1680 there were four cannon sited here and in the eighteenth century the Grand Battery was armed with fifteen 24-pound cannon which, in the event of an attack, combined with cannon fire from across the bay at St Aubin's Fort and the various batteries, towers and redoubts to completely cover the anchorage. The ten cannon that were left here in 1940 were removed by the Germans and so in the 1950s they were replaced by eight carronades made from the original moulds in the Carron Ironworks in Falkirk, Scotland.

Far Left and Right - The noonday gun.,
Below - The carronades.
Below Right - The Grand Battery complete with its 24-pounders in 1922.

The 'pepper pot' sentry box from the ditch.

Built into the side of the ditch are three magazines, which were used for storing gunpowder. These magazines were well protected and cool but very dark. Because soldiers were unable to use a candle or lamp to check the gunpowder supplies, oil lamps were placed behind a glass-window at the end of the long rooms. These were accessed by an outside corridor. The entrance to the magazine was protected by a curtain of wetted cloth or leather to prevent any sparks causing the gunpowder to ignite.

From the Ditch visitors get a good view of the 'pepper pot' sentry box perched on the angle of the salient. These were probably built during the 1730s and their shape is obviously influenced by those found in the Mediterranean where Britain had recently acquired possession of the Balearics and Gibraltar.

Head back up the steps and continue across the bridge, through the Third Gate and into the Lower Ward of the castle.

The storage of powder was always an issue in the castle. In 1783 there were 84 guns listed and if only half were used in the course of an attack, and each of these only fired 50 shots, then over 2,000 round shot and about 160 barrels (c.30 tons) of gunpowder would be used.

Lower Ward

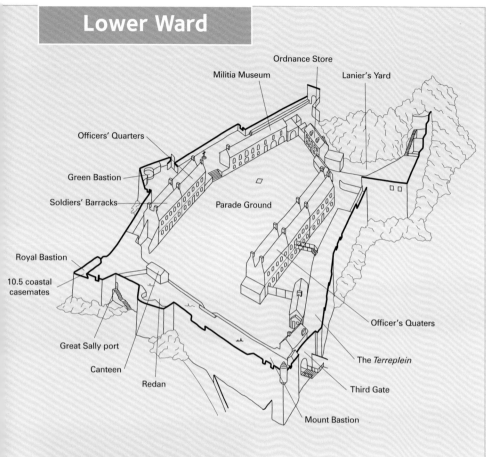

- Ordnance Store
- Militia Museum
- Lanier's Yard
- Officers' Quarters
- Green Bastion
- Soldiers' Barracks
- Parade Ground
- Royal Bastion
- 10.5 coastal casemates
- Great Sally port
- Canteen
- Redan
- Officer's Quaters
- The *Terreplein*
- Third Gate
- Mount Bastion

The approach to the Main Guard was a simple bridge set on granite pillars with a central rolling section but this was remodelled by Bastide in the 1730s and, although he rebuilt the curtain wall to the left of the gateway from the Mount Bastion to the Royal Bastion and added the 'pepper pot' sentry box, it appears he did little to change the gateway itself. The two-storey building to the right of and over the gateway is the only original 1636 building left in the Lower Ward although it was enlarged in 1749.

Just beyond the Main Guard on the right is a single-storey building which was built in the late eighteenth century to house the laundry, washrooms and a small bake house

Follow the stairs at the side of the Main Guard that lead up to the curtain wall - the raised platform behind the wall was known as the terreplein and this was where, in the period 1835-50, two traversing guns were sited.

LOWER WARD

This is the extent of the castle at the time of the English Civil War. Entered by the Third Gate, which was also known as the Main Guard when it was built about 1632, the Lower Ward was constructed in the period 1626-36 and enclosed the old monastic buildings and the Priory Church, which had been the focus of the islet for over five centuries.

Follow the path behind the Main Guard to the right and passing two splayed embrasures for carriage-mounted cannon you will reach the Mount Bastion. From here the East Curtain Wall, which was remodelled by Bastide in the 1730s, runs down to the Redan. In the masonry of the wall it is possible to pick out dressed stone reused from the Priory Church. The Redan originally had two cannon positions in each of its shorter sides and in the nineteenth century these were replaced by a traversing gun, the central pivot, running rails and low parapet all survive. In 1942 a concrete gun emplacement was placed here but all that survives of it is a small piece of concrete by the Redan Wall.

The paved area between the Redan and the Royal Bastion was a four-gun battery dominating the Havre St Jaume. The cannon fired through splayed embrasures in the parapet. The height of the wall has been greatly reduced and the decorated masonry thrown onto the beach below.

The Royal Bastion was originally an arrowhead-shaped bastion built in the 1630s and remodelled by Bastide in the 1730s, whose plan shows the walls pierced for eight cannon. However, it is very difficult to see anything of this today as the Occupying forces built another of the Jäger type coastal casemates over it. When they did this, they blocked access to the Great Sally Port which was via a long flight of stairs leading from the Lower Ward. The Great Sally Port is best seen either from the beach below the Walls or from the Redan.

From the Redan take the stairs into the Parade Ground.

Top - The central pivot of the nineteenth century traversing gun.

Above - The Great Sally Port, built in 1731 enabled the soldiers to use the garrison boat.

Left - The Mount Bastion.

The Parade Ground

In the seventeenth century the remains of the Priory Church dominated this area. Although the Tower was demolished in 1639, the nave stayed in use as the castle's chapel. Even though the building must have experienced extensive damage in the explosion of 1651, the building remained in constant use as a chapel, armoury, soldiers' lodgings and a garden throughout the rest of the century. Eventually everything was demolished and the stone re-used around the site. The last vestiges of the building must have disappeared when the Officers' Quarters were built in 1735.

Below - **The Officers' Quarters.**

Right - **The Parade Ground seen from the Mount.**

By the middle of the eighteenth century the Parade Ground had more or less assumed its present look. A large underground cistern was built to provide water storage and new buildings were put up around the Square. On the east side of the Square stand the Officers' Quarters built in 1735 and home for 12 officers. Senior officers had their own two-roomed apartments and junior officers had to double up. It now houses an exhibition entitled In War and Peace which tells the story of Elizabeth Castle. At the end of the building a Fives Court was added at the end of the eighteenth century. Fives was a ball game similar to squash but played with the hands instead of racquets and this is the last remaining example in Jersey. On the opposite side of the Square stand the Soldiers' Barracks, which took five years to build and were completed in 1755. In addition to the two storeys, there were also attic rooms lit by dormer windows but these were removed in 1949 when the building was re-roofed. In 1798 a report into the available accommodation showed that this building could accommodate up to 480 men as it had twelve rooms with nine double berths, twelve rooms with eight double berths and twelve 'garret' rooms for six men. Today it accommodates the café and an exhibition about the development of artillery and fortification – Granite and Gunpowder.

The Soldiers' Barracks.

At the south end of the Square is the Ordnance Store built in 1746. In 1755 it was described as a 'storehouse for dry provisions' and it has double doors and a projecting arm for a block-and-tackle fitted on the second floor. During the Occupation it was used as a kitchen for the German Garrison. Next to it is the Ablution Block built in the late nineteenth century.

Behind the Ablution Block is a narrow gateway leading into an area named Lanier's Yard named after a Sir John Lanier (1634-1692) who was Governor of the Castle between 1679 and 1684. Lanier's Magazine was built in 1682 and carries his coat of arms and date on the north wall, however, it was not well built and proved to be too damp and the powder needed to be stirred to keep it usable. Shuttered loopholes were added to the walls and this allowed a circulation of air which reduced the problem. The stone doorway is made from limestone and originally it may have been from the Priory Church. The lamp window can still be seen in the wall at the entrance and the floor would have been wooden. In the corner of the Yard the 1636 curtain wall ends in a Terraced Breastwork, built as gun platforms, up the side of the Mount towards the Upper Ward. The stonework includes re-used masonry from the Priory Church.

Below - The capped well in the Parade Ground. In 1800 a well was dug into the Square to supplement the water from the cisterns, but the water was described as 'brackish'. Soon after, the Board of Ordnance began the installation of rainwater tanks around the castle to supplement the supply.

This building on the southeast corner of the Square with the large arched windows, which now houses the Militia Museum, has a complex history. Essentially it is three separate buildings. At some stage in the late nineteenth century the central staircase was enclosed and for a while referred to as the Library Quarters. The area which was formerly the Gunner's Garden was enclosed and became the Library although by the end of the nineteenth century it was converted into a coach house. The Master Gunner's House

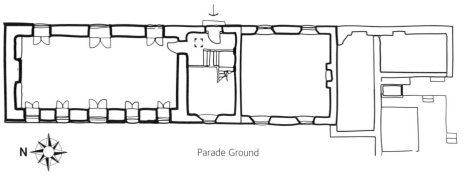

Parade Ground

? the northern end (the museum) was originally a storehouse and is marked down as such on both Philips' plan of 1680 and Bastide's plan of 1737:

? the central section was, in 1680, a staircase leading from the Square to the Upper Ward and in 1737 it was a flight of steps and the Master Gunner's Garden;

? the southern section, which was a two-storey workshop in 1680, had been converted into the Master Gunner's lodging by 1737.

retained its second storey and roof until the Occupation when it was semi-demolished. Today it stands as a roofless ruin. At some stage in the late eighteenth century, part of the building was referred to as the Blue Barracks. In 1798 it was reported that it could accommodate 124 men in one room with 25 double berths, a second room with 13 doubles and a third room with 24 double berths. This Blue Barrack had reputedly disappeared by 1842.

At the northern end of the Square stands the Canteen. Built in 1735 it was originally larger, but during the Occupation about one-third of it was demolished when the Occupying forces built the bunker to its right. They also obliterated any vestiges of the internal parts of the Great Sally Port. On the left hand side of the building there were cells built in 1737 but they lost their second storey when they were converted into a personnel shelter.

Above - The Canteen in November 1922 showing the full extent of the building.
Below left - The Canteen building today.

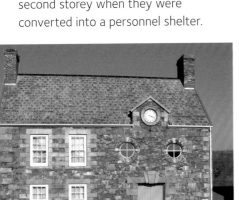

The Jäger type coastal casemate built into the Royal Bastion still contains its French-made Schneider 10.5 cm gun. Although the gun crew could not see what they were firing at, they could get an idea by looking at the range card painted above the gun embrasure. The gunner received instructions by telephone from the Fire Control Tower, which was built at the top of the castle. From this vantage point the commanding officer controlled the fire from the various gun positions around the castle. Bunkers such as this were made gas-tight and were equipped with ventilation pumps and extractor fans to pump out cordite fumes in the gunrooms. Food and bottled Vichy water were stored in special compartments. The soldiers in this bunker could survive for up to two months if it were sealed.

Left - The bunker entrance.
Below - The range card painted on the wall above the gun in the bunker.

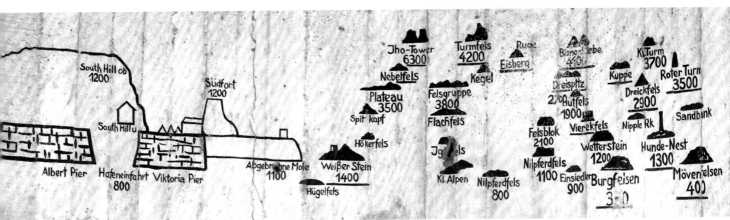

At the top of the stairs between the Officers Quarters and the Militia Museum stands a granite cross. This was erected in the centre of the Square in 1959 to mark the site of the High Altar of the Priory Church. However, recent research showed its positioning to be faulty and so the cross was moved to its present site to provide a visual link between the castle and the Oratory on the Hermitage Rock outside the walls. The curtain wall on this side of the castle follows its original 1626-36 alignment and, apart from some rebuilding of the top of the wall and additional stonework added against wave damage, is more or less original.

The arrowhead-shaped bastion by the cross is the Green Bastion built in the 1620s. Cannon placed here controlled the Inner Roads and the approaches to St Helier harbour. In 1737 it was shown to have four cannon placed in it and in the 1830s these were replaced by a traversing cannon. During the Occupation a machine gun emplacement for two guns and a flat top shelter for their crews were built into the tip of the 'arrowhead', while a floodlight was set up on the gun position itself. This lit up the approaches to the harbour but in order to do so part of the parapet had to be reduced, although it was rebuilt in the 1980s on health and safety grounds. Associated with this were two concrete personnel shelters half buried in the ground to the rear of the Officers' Quarters.

Towards the Royal Bastion at the rear of the Officers' Quarters are two more 1830s traversing gun positions, one of which was modified in 1942 by the Germans to take a machine gun position. The rails in both are still visible.

In the curtain wall just beyond the Cross is another 1942 machine gun position with a concrete blast wall and shelter built into a small eighteenth century square turret. From this position the visitor gets a good view over the wall of the tank turret set into concrete at the base of the curtain wall of Ralegh's Yard in the Upper Ward. This is a Renault tank turret and is one of about 60 captured French tank turrets that were brought to the Island and used as fixed gun positions. They were mounted on a 'Ringstand' – a toothed rail set into concrete.

Follow the curtain wall to reach the Iron Gate at its southern end. This was the entrance to the original Elizabeth Castle, the oldest part of the castle comprising the 1594-1601 work of Paul Ivy, the Queen's Engineer, and the 1600-03 extensions made by Sir Walter Raleigh[7].

"... presumed to christen it ... Fort Isabella Bellissima ..."

Sir Walter Raleigh, 1600

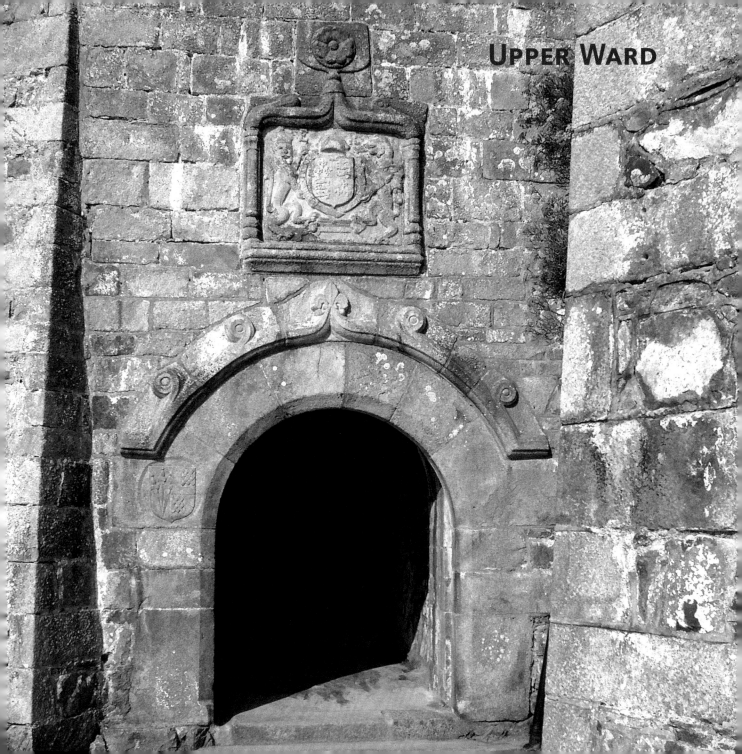

Upper Ward

The Upper Ward has always been the most heavily defended part of the castle and has been continuously repaired and remodelled form its earliest days until the German Occupation.

The Iron Gate was built around 1600 as part of the first extension work. It was protected from direct assault by a small enclosure that had another gateway set at a right-angle to it. The remains of this can still be seen. A guardroom to the left of the gate has a small gun embrasure set into it, which would have housed a small 'murderer' or cannon commanding the approaches to the gate. Above the arch the empty niche should have had a Royal coat of arms set into it, but this failed to materialise, possibly when Sir Walter Raleigh was removed from office by King James I.

The gatehouse lost its room above the arch in the nineteenth century when much of this area was remodelled. The actual entrance arch with its massive shoulder stones[8] is typically Jersey in style.

Sometimes referred to as the Fourth Gate, the Iron Gate gave access via a covered stairway to Ralegh's Yard. This was originally built as a gun platform or terreplein with a triangular bastion as an extra defence outside the Queen Elizabeth Gate. It might have been named after Sir Walter Raleigh, however, a George Ralegh was Lieutenant Governor here in 1661. Throughout the eighteenth and nineteenth centuries a number of buildings were put up in the area. In 1844 they were described as the Staff Sergeant's Quarters. Partly demolished during the Occupation, a party of German POWs completely removed the ruined buildings in 1946.

Facing page - This archive photograph of the Iron Gate, taken in 1922, is interesting in that it shows the number of Victorian buildings in Ralegh's Yard that were demolished in the late 1920s and during the Occupation.

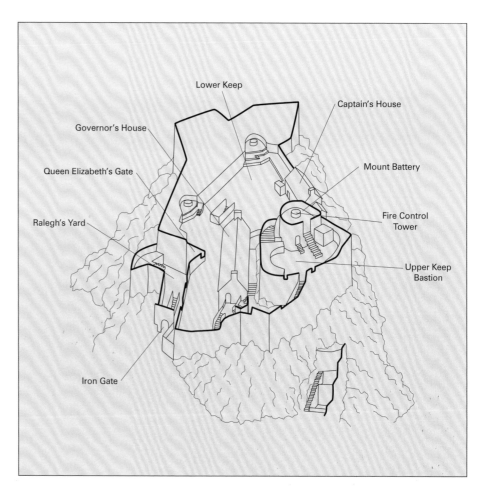

A raised platform was built on the triangular bastion at the southern end of Raleigh's Yard during the Occupation. Originally a heavy machine gun was placed here but this was replaced with a searchlight when the tank turret was positioned at the base of the wall overlooking the breakwater. The searchlight, code-named *Anton*, served *Batterie Endrass* at Westmount by picking out targets.

Set into the walls is the original entrance to the castle, the Queen Elizabeth Gate, built in the 1590s. This is a monument to the skill of Paul Ivy. The angle of the wall – slanting inwards to the advantage of those defending the castle – forced the enemy into a difficult position where it would be relatively easy to pick them off with cannon fire. The carving above the arch was possibly done by Peter Bisson who carried out a similar set of carvings at Mont Orgueil in 1593. Beneath a large Tudor rose are the arms of Elizabeth I whose initials flank the crown. In the centre are the Royal Arms encircled by the Garter. The supporters are the lion of England and the dragon of Wales while on the left are the arms of Sir Anthony Paulet[9], the Governor of the day.

Above – The arms of Sir Anthony Paulet.

Left – The arms of Elizabeth I.

Opposite page, left – 6.5 inch RML (Rifled Muzzle Loader)

As one enters the Queen Elizabeth Gate the portcullis slots are plainly visible in the sides of the arch. These indicate that there must have been a chamber directly above the gate which has been covered over or filled in. When Ivy built the castle, solid walls were built directly onto the rock and a gun platform was constructed on the summit. This enclosed area was the Lower Keep. Projecting out from this central space were three demi-bastions connected by curtain walls. This was the fortress named by Sir Walter Raleigh in honour of his Queen - Fort Isabella Bellissima.

At the head of the stairs is a cannon that is sunk into the ground. This was used as a fixed point on which to secure a block and tackle to haul heavy loads up the stairs.

The concrete building to the left was originally built in 1900 as a personnel shelter for the gun crews who served the two 4.7 inch guns that were positioned in the barbettes on either side of it. These have shell recesses or expense magazines associated with them. The personnel shelter lost its windows, doors and wooden floors during the Occupation when the two barbette pedestals were adapted to take 2.0 cm Flak 38 guns. Prior to 1900 this area was a three-gun emplacement, which had been built in the first half of the nineteenth century – possibly between 1835 and 1850. These guns would have been traversing guns with a central pivot point and rails for the carriages as can be seen at other positions around the castle. Records show that the guns would have been 7 inch RMLs (Rifled Muzzle Loaders) – similar to the one shown in the Granite and Gunpowder exhibition.

The oldest building in the Lower Keep is the Captain's House. This was where the castle commander or captain originally lived and the date 1594 can still be seen on the surviving chimney. Apart from the kitchen with its open fire and small bread oven, little remains of the house as about three-quarters of the building was cut down about 1700 to provide a gun platform overlooking the anchorage in the bay to the west. The tops of five window arches can still be seen in the low wall of the platform. The cellar was converted into a magazine and shell store in the nineteenth century about the same time the three-gun emplacement was created. While the magazine is reached by the covered stairs, stores could be hoisted up and lowered down via the shaft next to the stairs.

From this point there are two routes to the summit of the castle either up the stairs to the south of the Governor's House or by the stairs to the north. The first route leads past the mason's mark cut into the rock face on the right and to the magazine adjoining the Captain's House. Although this does not feature on Paul Ivy's 1594 plan it appears to have been built onto an existing arrowhead bastion. An inventory of 1617 records 41 barrels of gunpowder stored here and it is shown on the 1680s plan, so it is safe to assume that it is an early feature of the Lower Keep defences. The garderobes or lavatories, which are reached by a short passage next to the magazines, appear to be ancient but are essentially Victorian.

Below – The Captain's House

The first Governor to live here was Sir Water Raleigh in 1600, although in his three-year tenure he only spent 13 weeks in the Island. The two arms on each side of the archway belong to William Fortescue and John Wadham who we presume were involved in the building of Elizabeth Castle.

In 1646 when Prince Charles arrived with his entourage of 300 to take up residence in the castle he would have lived here in the Governor's House. He later returned as King Charles II in 1649 along with his brother, the Duke of York.

In the 1730s a third storey was added and the whole building was rendered with cement. In 1842 the third floor was used as the castle chapel and remained as such until the castle lost its military role. In the late 1920s and 1930 the building was taken back to its seventeenth century appearance. The third floor was taken away and the cement render removed, the chimneys and the gable ends were rebuilt, the porches on the two ground floor doors were demolished and the windows were restored to their original proportions, and the whole of the internal woodwork was renewed. During the Occupation, the Germans used it as a barracks but their alterations were all removed in 1946.

Governer's House before and after restoration in 1929

The second route passes in front of the Governor's House. This building is typical of Jersey architecture of the late sixteenth century. It has two floors, each with two rooms; however, it also has a basement and cistern in the northern end. As the house is built into the Mount, when it rains the water runs down the rock-face in the basement. The builders used this to their advantage by cutting a channel into the back wall which leads the water into the cistern.

According to plans produced in 1680, 1737 and 1880 there were buildings in front of the Governor's House but these were demolished and the height of the wall adjusted in the late nineteenth century. A cistern was also sunk here to supplement the water supplies in the late eighteenth century.

The steps to the north of the Governor's House lead up to the Upper Keep Redoubt. At the first landing a small square guardroom was built in the first decades of the eighteenth century. The steps continue to the Upper Keep Bastion where Paul Ivy's plan shows one cannon positioned. In the period 1835-50 a traversing gun was sited here and an associated magazine was built, cut into the rock beneath the Mount Battery. It was possibly at this time that the present staircase leading up to the Upper Keep itself was built. Prior to this the stairs had led up around a lofty look-out tower, built about 1630, which jutted out from the north east point of the wall – today this is marked simply by a rock outcrop at the head of the steps.

The Upper Keep surmounted by the German Fire Control Tower seen from the seaward side.

Both routes join again here on the Upper Keep. This was originally the site of a gun platform built in 1551, and was essentially an open space, like a shell keep, enclosed by high walls. Ivy's Plan of 1594 shows four cannon housed here, while in 1737 Bastide shows the walls pierced by sixteen loopholes for cannon. In 1680 this was referred to as The Mount, while in 1737 it was known as the Upper Saluting Platform and in 1755 simply as the Saluting Platform, because this was where cannon fired salutes to visiting warships. At some stage during the eighteenth century the height of both the walls and the lookout tower were reduced and in the early Victorian period the top of the Upper Keep was modified and two traversing guns were placed here. Today only one of the positions is still visible with its two rails still intact, along with the low barbette wall and the shell recess. The other is buried beneath the Fire Control Tower which now dominates the top of the Upper Keep. This was a two level structure in that the inside allowed the Germans to co-ordinate the fire from the various gun positions around the castle while the top of the tower could be used in fair weather for spotting targets. The concrete plinth in the centre was the mounting for the third of the 2.0cm Flak 38 guns of the anti-aircraft battery known as IV Zug.

From the tower the views are extensive – all along the south east coast of the Island and down as far south as the Minquiers. Any vessels approaching from the east and the south could be spotted immediately, while signal stations sited on Noirmont and Corbière gave warnings of anything approaching from the west.

Meanwhile, over to the east, and dominating the skyline over St Helier and the harbour is Fort Regent, Elizabeth Castle's successor as the Island's principal fortress. Work began on this in 1806 and by 1814 it was ready to take over.

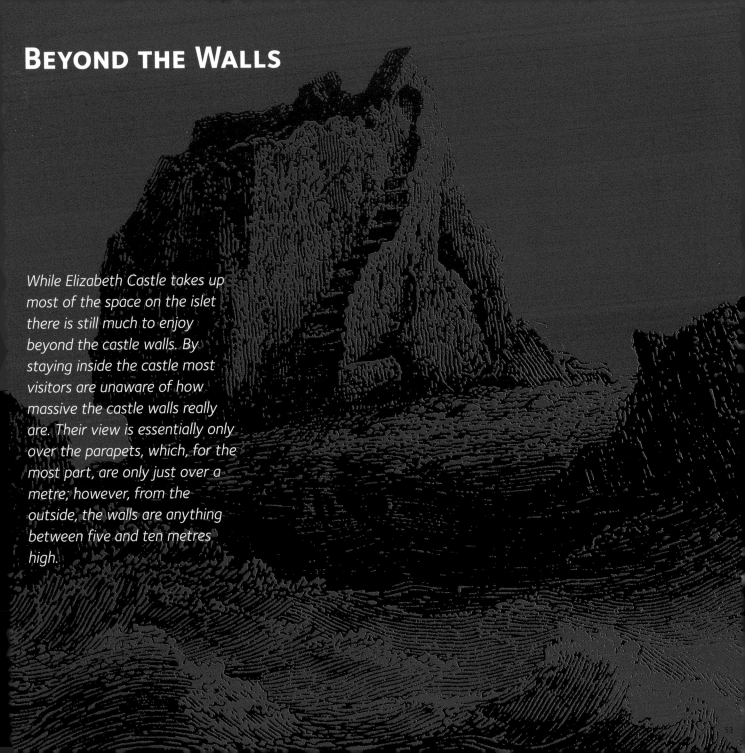

BEYOND THE WALLS

While Elizabeth Castle takes up most of the space on the islet there is still much to enjoy beyond the castle walls. By staying inside the castle most visitors are unaware of how massive the castle walls really are. Their view is essentially only over the parapets, which, for the most part, are only just over a metre; however, from the outside, the walls are anything between five and ten metres high.

When the oratory was being restored in the 1930s, traces of a fresco were uncovered in the southwest corner of the building.

When Helier was killed in 555AD by a band of pirates, local legend said that he picked up his head and walked for 200 steps. A small community of monks built a church close by and the area became a place of pilgrimage. Helier's death is commemorated on the parish crest which features a pair of crossed axes. Every year on the Sunday nearest to St Helier's Day, 16 July, the parish authorities organise a procession to lay a wreath at the entrance to the oratory.

Left and below- The Hermitage

Facing page above - The Hermitage Rock with its oratory and gun battery. The remains of the Blacksmith's Shop can be seen to the left.

Facing page below - The low water landing stage beneath the Royal Bastion.

The Hermitage

The town of St Helier was named after the sixth century hermit who came to Jersey from the area we now call Belgium, seeking an isolated spot where he could devote his life to prayer and fasting. The rock, on which he found solitude and where he lived for 15 years, still stands about 200 metres to the south west of the Green Bastion in the Lower Ward and is known as the Hermitage Rock. Whereas in Helier's time, it was separated from the islet by the tide, today it is connected by the nineteenth century harbour works.

The actual rock ledge, on which Helier was supposed to have slept, known as St Helier's Bed, was covered over by a small chapel or oratory during the twelfth century. The walls are made of granite rubble and the vaulted roof is made from flat stones set into mortar. It is approached from the breakwater by a very steep set of stairs.

The Gun Battery

About 1678, during the governorship of Sir Thomas Morgan (1665-1679), a gun battery or breastwork was built on top of the Hermitage Rock and the Oratory was pressed into service as a guardhouse. A report in 1680 recorded that the position was armed with a couple of 3-pounders in the battery and the Oratory housed a falconet[10]. Although the position was abandoned in the mid-eighteenth century, traces of the stonework still survive.

The Harbour Works

The small harbour between the castle and the Hermitage Rock was built in the 1870s when the States, the Island government, accepted Sir John Coode's plan to create a deep water harbour for St Helier by building piers out from La Collette on the one side and the Hermitage Rock on the other.

The small harbour beneath the castle walls was built to accommodate this work. The harbour itself, built between the castle and the Hermitage Rock, handled the rocks imported onto the islet. The reclaimed land behind it was used for site buildings and, more importantly, to make the concrete blocks required for the project, which were made in a pit behind the harbour beneath the castle walls. Rock barges brought the raw material out to the islet where they were unloaded, either by crane onto the pier or else over the side of the barge into waiting carts at low tide which were then hauled up a slipway – traces of which can still be seen in the arch in the corner of the harbour.

The foundation stone was laid in August 1872 and work began, but construction costs began to spiral and the next year the Island experienced a bank crash which knocked confidence. The Island's merchant fleet shrank and so the

project was abandoned in 1876 with the Elizabeth Castle breakwater having been partially built and the La Collette arm, which should have been pushed out to the rock called the Dog's Nest, abandoned as just a stump. A second attempt to complete the job occurred in 1887 when the castle arm was extended by about 150 metres but still had to stop 150 metres short of the Platte Rock. Nevertheless, the resulting breakwater did protect the Inner Roads and the entrance to St Helier harbour from the southwesterly gales.

The Garrison boat in the Havre de St Jaume, 1903.

The area around the harbour was a bustling settlement of workshops and storage but today only one building stands up to its full height. This is a single storey building about 15 metres by 7 metres, close to the head of the slipway, known popularly as the Blacksmith's Shop. Behind it amongst the rocks there are a number of solid structures, which represent low water landing stages which could ne used by the workmen as the tide dropped. Nestling under the Hermitage Rock just behind the Blacksmith's Shop are the ruined remains of a small stone magazine that was associated with the building of the breakwater.

A similar arrangement of low granite walls and concrete levels set amongst the rocks can still be seen beneath the Royal Bastion. These are the military low water stages, built in the eighteenth century, that were accessed from Le Havre de Saint Jaume by the Great Sally Port. It was from here that the garrison boat plied its trade between the castle and the harbour.

The massive cube of concrete at the base of the Hermitage Rock housed an anti-tank gun and machine gun and also held the control panel for the electrically detonated minefield which protected the Inner Roads and the entrance to the harbour. This was one of a pair – the other is on the other side of the Inner Roads at La Collette.

Glossary

barbette - the name comes from the French phrase *en barbette* referring to the practice of firing cannon over a parapet rather than through an embrasure. A barbette allows better angles of fire but gives the gun crews less protection than the latter.

bastion - a strongpoint projecting from the walls to cover dead ground and to provide crossfire.

battery - an emplacement for cannon.

casemate - a fortified gun emplacement.

curtain wall - a wall enclosing the castle. Most often it was attached to the towers and gatehouses.

embrasure - a splayed opening in a wall or parapet.

gatehouse - the strongpoint designed to house, protect and defend the gateway.

magazine - a strengthened storeroom for gunpowder and arms.

parade ground - a square used by soldiers for drills and inspection.

parapet - a protective wall on outer side of the wall walk.

redan - a V-shaped salient angle projecting out in the direction of an expected attack.

sally port - a small, narrow gate or a secondary gateway.

terreplein - the fighting platform on which various types of guns and emplacements are sited.

traverse wall (also known as a cross wall) - an internal wall dividing the castle into separate areas.

wall walk - a walkway on top of a wall, protected by a parapet.

Notes

pg 22 [1] A demi-culverin fired a nine-pound shot and had a range of just over 1600m although its effective range was only about 80m.

[2] a saker fired a solid iron shot weighing between four and six pounds.

pg 25 [3] A minion fired a three-pound round shot.

pg 26 [4] Thomas Philips was a military engineer who accompanied Lieutenant-Colonel George Legge to the Island in 1679-80.

pg 28 [5] Philippe Dumaresq, Survey of the Island of Jersey, 1685.

pg 33 [6] Fortress standard meant that it was constructed with reinforced concrete walls and roof two metres thick and capable of withstanding heavy and sustained bombardment.

pg 44 [7] Sir Walter Raleigh (1552-1618) was Governor of Jersey, between 1600 and 1603. Raleigh's name can be found spelled in over 70 different ways in contemporary documents. He, himself, signed it in a variety of ways, finally settling on "Ralegh" — bizarrely enough Raleigh himself never spelled it with an "i".

pg 46 [8] A shoulder stone is the stone from which an arch starts.

pg 47 [9] Sir Anthony Paulet (1562-1600) - the son of Sir Amyas Paulet and Margaret Hervey, was made Lieutenant Governor in 1583 and was sworn in as Governor in 1590. He died in 1600 and was succeeded by Sir Walter Raleigh.

pg 55 [10] A falconet fired a round shot weighing just over a pound.

First published Jersey 2008

By Jersey Heritage
Jersey Museum, The weighbridge, St Helier,
Jersey, JE2 3NF

ISBN 978-0-9552508-5-9

Text copyright © Jersey Heritage
Illustrations © individuals and organisations
credited

Plans © Jersey Heritage

Acknowledgements

The author would like to thank the
following people for their help, advice and
contribution of material for this souvenir
guide: the "bold corps" of Elizabeth Castle
re-enactors, gardiens past and present, and
all his colleagues from Jersey Heritage who
supported him during its writing, especially
Wayne Audrain for the design and the late
Mel Warrs (1952-2007) for his unfailing
assistance.

Picture Credits

Photographs supplied by:
Stuart Abraham, Robin Briault, Gordon Collas, Doug Ford, Sven Ford, Cassie Horton,
John Lord, Neil Mahrer

British Library
        8 & 44, Royal 18 D. III Jersey Harbour, manuscript plan ref *Lord Burghley's Atlas*
        9, Cotton Augustus I.i Drawing by Paul Ivy
        44, 9005.h.2 portrait of Sir Walter Raleigh ref *The Historie of the World
        In five bookes.* Sam Cartwright

Bundesarchiv 17

Jersey Heritage/Société Jersiaise Collection 5, 6, 10, 11, 12, 13, 14, 15, 18, 30, 31 & 53

Further Information

Aldsworth, F (2005): *Elizabeth Castle Conservation Plan – part 1*
Balleine, GR (1976): *All for the King*
Brown, M (1986): *Elizabeth Castle, Jersey*
Cooms, D (2005): *Elizabeth Castle – just off the coast of Jersey (unpublished)*
Ginns, W (1980): *Jersey Besieged*
Jamieson, AG (1986): *A People of the Sea*
Rybot, NVL (1934): *Elizabeth Castle*
Rybot, NVL (1948): *The Islet of St Helier and Elizabeth Castle, Jersey*

Opposite - 'Charming Betty', the amphibious castle ferry named after a local 18th century privateering ship.